you and your
JACK RUSSELL
PUPPY

in a
nutshell

The essential owners' guide to perfect puppy
parenting – with easy-to-follow steps on how
to choose and care for your new arrival

Carry Aylward

NUTSHELL
BOOKS

ISBN: 978-1-9161897-0-6

Front cover design by Nutshell Books
Book design by Nutshell Books
Photography: Carry Aylward, © Shutterstock,
© Dreamstime

Printed by Amazon

First printed 2019

Nutshell Books
3 Holmlea Road, Goring on Thames
RG8 9EX, United Kingdom
www.nutshell-books.com

*To you, the reader, to the Jack Russell
you choose, and to the special times
you will share*

CONTENTS

FOREWORD

How exciting that you're considering a puppy from such a characterful breed, and congratulations on taking this step towards being an excellent owner. Whether or not you've had a Jack Russell before, you've chosen the perfect starter guide for puppy parents-to-be.

This book answers the most important early-stage questions, and leads you step by step through the process – from deciding whether a Jack Russell is right for you, to the first days, and through the subsequent weeks and months (the all-important formative time when your puppy is growing and learning at its fastest).

This handbook is intentionally concise, bringing together up-to-date research in an easy-to-read, easy-to-follow format that gives you only what you need to know, when you need to know it.

Also, and purely for the sake of easy reading, your puppy is referred to as 'he' throughout, but please consider 'he' to mean 'she or he' in every instance.

The advice in this book will help you to build a solid foundation for a wonderful relationship with your Jack Russell. It is meant to keep you smiling through the love and cuddles as well as the puddles and poops, heart-wrenching nights and shredded items of value.

All you need now is to brace yourself with unconditional love and a good sense of humour.

Let's get started.

1. IS A JACK RUSSELL RIGHT FOR YOU?

Decisions, decisions!

If you're undecided about a puppy, and more specifically a Jack Russell, this chapter will help you make a more informed decision.

Almost all dog owners think their own dog's breed is the best. But there's a saying, 'Once you've had a Jack, you'll never go back' and, as a third-time Jack Russell owner, I speak with confident bias when I say that Jack Russells really are the very best.

All puppies are cute, but Jack Russells have a special kind of cuteness. Just think how often they are featured in films, TV shows, advertisements, brochures ... they are chosen over and over again. I rest my case.

But before we dip into the cute, and not-so-cute, characteristics of Jack Russells, let's run though some quick but important general questions. Because choosing a dog is a momentous decision!

If you are new to owning a dog, any dog, when you invite one into your world, your life will never be the same. You will soon start thinking differently about what you wear, the places you visit, your holiday destinations, the car you drive and, yes, even your next house. Your life will also be warmer, stinkier, happier ... richer in so many ways.

But are you really ready for a dog?

If you invite a dog into your home, he should be treated like family. Ask yourself very honestly whether, at this time in your life, and for the next 15-plus years, you will be able to give him the love, time, space, care and patience he deserves. No dog should ever be cast aside like a pair of shoes its owner has grown tired of.

Is a puppy right for you?

Ask yourself honestly whether you can face the puppy stage with the pooping, weeing and chewing of everything in sight. If not, you might consider taking on an older dog, one that has finished with toilet training, teething and even adolescence.

Do you value the quiet life?

Have you considered giving a home to a dog in its senior years? There are so many beautiful creatures that need re-homing through no fault of their own, and if you are no longer as active as you once were, this might be the best choice for you now.

Do you have other pets?

If you have other dogs or cats, consider carefully how a puppy would fit in to your family. If you get your Jack Russell as a small puppy, there's no reason for him to be a problem with your other pets. Your other pets, however, might not be quite so adaptable.

Do you have small children?

If you have children too small to understand how they might be hurting a puppy when they pull his tail or ears, or carry him around, then it might be better to get an older dog, or a larger breed, or to wait a few years. Many small dogs aren't good with small children, but if a Jack Russell is not good with them, he has most likely had bad experiences as a puppy.

You still want a puppy?

I know. They are warm and cuddly and there's nothing as sweet as the pitter patter of puppy feet. But the first steps to getting a puppy are a big investment – not just financially, but also in terms of time, energy and emotion. This is not an effort to put you off getting a dog. Quite the opposite. It is just really important that you are sure you are able to give your puppy the happy life it deserves and fully understand the commitment you are making. Too many dogs are re-homed, and even put down, each year because their owners underestimated the responsibility.

Finally back to Jack Russells

So if you're sure about a puppy and considering a Jack Russell, let's look a little more at the specifics of the breed. Besides being the best, cutest, most beguiling dogs I've ever known, they are also very loving. They are playful; they are deeply devoted to their owners; they are highly intelligent. They are brave, feisty, energetic, adventurous and the list goes on. They can make incredibly rewarding pets.

BUT …
(and note that was a big 'BUT'), they are not for everyone. Being a Jack Russell owner is no doddle.

They are bright little buttons
While it's safe to assume that everyone wants their dog to be loving, playful and devoted, believe it or not, not everyone wants a dog that is quite so intelligent. Jack Russells are often accused of being too smart; intelligent beyond their 'station in life'. Pair this with their feisty natures and you've got a breed that is rewarding and challenging in equal measure.

You need to accept this gracefully, or brace yourself and be prepared – and this book will tell you how to do that – because if you're not careful, your sweet, adoring puppy will have you wrapped around his little paw-kins before you know it.

Jack Russells also have very good memories, and that applies to the things that go right as well as the things that go wrong. They pick up good habits quickly, and bad ones just as fast. So with a Jack Russell it is especially important to be an excellent puppy parent from day one. You need to set clear rules, and to be particularly consistent in training, and the chapter on Behaviour focuses on both of these.

Courageous

Jack Russells also tend to be brave beyond their size. They will happily play, fight or play fight, with dogs several times bigger than themselves which, for a loving and devoted owner, can be a little hair-raising at times. (See 'George' in the penultimate chapter on Standout Jack Russells.)

Active

Above all, they are energetic. Whoever coined the phrase, 'dynamite comes in small packages' probably had a Jack Russell. They need exercise and love the outdoors. The first dog to visit both the North and South Poles was Bothy, a Jack Russell who belonged to renowned explorers Ranulph and Ginny Fiennes.

Big on the inside

They are basically big dogs in small, compact bodies. I think it's great that you can scoop your big-little dog into your arms if and when you need to. And if you've got an enclosed garden or yard, they're an ideal size for a pet-flap in the door.

Need stimulation

But small and portable as they are, Jack Russells are no handbag or designer dogs. They need mental and physical stimulation. If you shut them inside on their own for long stretches, don't be surprised if they try to get out – and they're talented escape artists – or to redesign your favourite armchair. They can destroy things because they're upset with you, need more attention or are bored, and you'll only have yourself to blame.

Characters

Jack Russells are great at getting into trouble. They are cheeky little monkeys with larger-than-life personalities and they can't help their naughty little selves. But that's also why we like them so much, so if you choose a Jack Russell, bear that in mind when he pushes the limits.

Tenacious

Almost all dogs were originally bred for some aspect of hunting. Terriers were bred for hunting small prey and Jack Russells, more specifically, for sniffing out foxes and pulling and chasing them from their holes. This is why they are strong, determined, enjoy digging and love rooting around for toys.

Better than you think

Don't underestimate them. Whatever you believe about your Jack Russell, the likelihood is that he is ahead of the game. He can jump higher (up to five times his own height), run further, chew harder, and get through smaller spaces than you might believe possible. He knows what you're thinking, feeling and planning for next week, and he knows all your secrets. (It's a good thing he can't talk.)

Bottom line

Every Jack Russell has his own charming personality and sometimes less charming traits. But picture this as a very-worst-case scenario: he might run after small prey and not listen when you call him back; fight with big dogs; take himself on his own walks (if you didn't, and he wanted to and could get out); snap at small children and/or chew your household items. But if you can give him love and attention, keep him active and busy – mentally and physically, and if you can give him playtime, toys and walks, you needn't ever experience any of these. You will have fun beyond measure. And those little paws will make the biggest footprints in your heart.

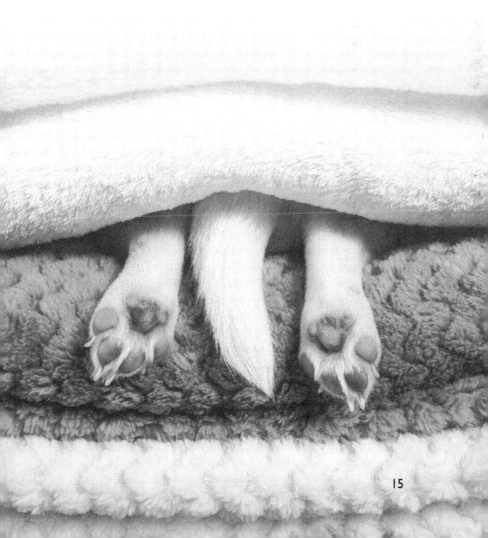

2. HOW TO FIND YOUR PUPPY

You've decided you want a Jack Russell puppy, and I'm thrilled for you. There are wonderful, magical, hilarious, sock-nicking, poo-picking, finger-nipping, chin-licking times ahead. And more love than you could ever imagine.

It could be that you're happy with the first Jack Russell that comes your way, but if you're sniffing around seeking out available puppies you might as well start by sorting out some preferences in your own mind. No two Jack Russells are the same, so look out for them when you're out and about. Look at pictures in books and online, and work out what type of Jack Russell you'd like – what shape, size, and combination of colour, and whether you'd prefer a girl or a boy.

Unless you live alone, make sure that you involve all members of the family and household in these decisions. It's very important that everyone has bought into the whole idea from the very start. The more say the whole family has in choosing the dog, the more likely they will be to actively engage with and care for it, and the less likely they'll be to shirk their dog-walking, poo-picking responsibilities.

CONSIDERATIONS

Strains of the breed

If you are unclear about the difference between the Parson Russell terrier, the Jack Russell terrier and the Russell terrier you are not alone. They are all strains of the same breed and can be easily confused. The specific distinctions of the different strains are beyond the need-to-know parameters of a this book, but in a nutshell:

- **The Parson Russell** has the largest overall body size and longest legs, giving it more of a square shape in profile.
- **The Jack Russell** – also sometimes called the English Jack Russell terrier or the Short Jack Russell terrier – is generally a smaller dog. It is also more rectangular in its proportions, with shorter legs in relation to its body.
- **The Russell terrier** shares the shorter-legs and longer body proportions of the Jack Russell, but is smaller still.

Purebred and pedigrees

Many puppy farmers and backyard breeders mate their dogs with other breeds, and still advertise them as Jack Russells. Although these puppies might grow into lovely dogs, they are unlikely to have the traits of a true Jack Russell. Again this is up to you, but if you do want a purebred Jack Russell – meaning its parents are of the same breed – it is important that you see the mother and, if it's not possible to meet the father, that you at least see photos of him.

Despite being such a popular pet for well over 100 years, in the United Kingdom – where it was originally bred – the Jack Russell was only finally recognised as a pedigree dog breed in 2016. If you want a pedigree Jack Russell – a purebred dog that is also registered with a recognised breed association or society such as the Kennel Club – you must choose a puppy from a breeder that is a registered member of one of these societies.

And if you are planning to show your dog or become a registered breeder yourself, you will certainly need to do more research. The section 'Useful Information' at the end of the book has a list of organisations and websites you can refer to.

Coat

Jack Russells by whatever name can be smooth coated, rough (or wiry) coated, or broken coated (which is a combination of the two), so if you have a preference this will help to narrow your search.

All the coat types shed throughout the year and need regular grooming, but rough coats also need hand shedding every five to six months. For this you can use a dog grooming professional or do it yourself with a stripping knife (which doesn't actually cut the fur). There are plenty of excellent 'how to' demonstrations on YouTube.

Colour

Jack Russells are white with patches of tan or black, or a combination of the two. The tan can vary from lemon tan (a light, bright brown) through to red tan (a rich, warm brown) and sable tan (a deep brown). A puppy with white, black and tan is tri-coloured. Deciding on the colour of the markings can also narrow your search. If it's important to you for your dog's markings to be close to the breeding standard then, as a quick guide, and across all strains of the breed, white should be dominant and patches or spots should ideally be around the head and the root of the tail (where the tail joins the body).

Shape

Leg length and roundness of frame vary. If body shape is important to you, decide which you prefer. In my experience, many casual or unregistered breeders won't be able to answer you on this level of specifics and, if this is the case, you should look to the mother and father, or photos of the father, for an indication of how the puppies are likely to turn out.

Girl or boy?

Honestly, that's up to you. Unless you're wanting to use your dog for breeding purposes someday, I don't believe there's much in it, especially if you're planning on having it spayed or neutered. (There is more on neutering in the chapter 'Going forward'.)

Tails

All Jack Russells with short tails have been docked. This means a portion of their tail has been removed, most likely in the first week after birth. Decades ago there were several practical reasons for this, but these days it's mainly done for cosmetic purposes.

As a result, tail docking has been banned or restricted in many parts of the world. For example in the United Kingdom only Jack Russells that are certified to be working dogs can be legally docked. In the United States and parts of Canada, however, it's still a fairly common practice.

TIMING

As well as getting an idea of the sort of puppy you're looking for, you need to decide on the best time to bring your puppy into your family. This should be at the beginning of a stretch when most of the family will be home and able to care for the puppy full-time for most of the day. If you are retired this might not be a consideration, but if you are a working family with school-going children, for example, you should try to pick your puppy up early in the school holidays.

The weather is another consideration. If you live in a country where the summer and winter temperatures are very different, and the wet and dry seasons vary, then getting your puppy at the start of a warm or dry season will make for much easier toilet training.

Luckily any sensible breeder in your area is likely to have taken these facts into consideration, so you will find that the most puppies are available at the start of summer and the long school holidays.

Generally good breeders will also not let their puppies go to their new homes before they are eight or nine weeks old. Ideally you want to visit the litter and meet the puppies around the six-week mark.

The next step then is to decide the date when it will

be most convenient for you to take the puppy home. Eight weeks before that date you can start looking for new litters.

Ideally the very first step of all is to identify the best route to finding puppies for sale in your area. This might be a kennel club, a publication, a website or a combination of options. (Males are often advertised on websites for breeding, and if you see a male you particularly like you could ask the owner to keep you informed of new litters he has fathered.) This research will also give you a sense of when puppies are advertised and what they look like when they are newborn and very young. Some people advertise their litters very early, and some only when the puppies are almost ready to go to their forever homes.

BUYING RESPONSIBLY

There is an alarming amount of puppy farming going on out there (as well as right here under our noses). Puppy farmers are high volume breeders who breed puppies with little or no consideration for the health and wellbeing of the puppies or their parents. Intent on profit, they ignore guidelines on the safe maximum number of litters per dog, and typically separate puppies from their mothers too early (before the recommended age of eight weeks). The mothers and puppies live in conditions ranging from substandard to awful, then the puppies are moved to normal-looking homes for viewings – homes which are, in reality, nothing more than a shop front.

So when arranging to see a litter, please make sure it's with a responsible breeder. You want to be certain you are buying a healthy, happy puppy and, at the same time, not unknowingly supporting the cruel puppy trade.

Puppy farmers and dealers can be tricky to identify, but these are some of the telltale signs that should make you think twice.

The advert

- Puppy farmers often use the same contact number on more than one advert. If the advert is posted on the internet, do a search on the number see if it has been used on any other puppy adverts.
- They often use the same descriptions, word-for-word, in more than one advert. Search a key phrase in the wording to locate duplicate advertising.
- Photos of the puppies may also have been used on other adverts. Right click on the photo, then select 'search Google for image' to find out.
- A vet will not vaccinate a puppy before four weeks of age so if a person is advertising a vaccinated puppy that is three weeks old, stay away.
- Don't be fooled by promises of 'free puppy packs'. These don't make the sellers any more legitimate.
- If the breeder claims to be Kennel Club registered, check this with the Kennel Club.

First contact

Now to make the call. (Emailing is your next best option but you will learn so much more by speaking to the breeder in person.) These are some key questions to ask:

- Did you breed the puppies yourself?

    It's imperative they did so you can meet the mother.

- Are the puppies currently in the place where they were bred?

That is where you need to see the litter.

- How many puppies are, or were there, in the litter?

  It's always best to see the puppies together so you can compare them and see how they interact. Avoid seeing just one.

- Have the puppies or their mother had any health problems?

- Have they been treated for worms?

  Ideally the puppies will have received at least one worming treatment from the breeder.

- Have they been given their first vaccinations?

  Vaccination requirements vary from country to country, but initial vaccinations generally comprise two doses with an interval of two to four weeks. The first of these is usually given before eight weeks of age, but not before three to four weeks.

- Have they been microchipped?

  This is a tiny chip injected under your puppy's skin at the back of his neck. It holds his unique number which links to your contact details and, unlike a collar and tag, it stays there for life. If they have been microchipped that's a bonus, but it's not essential. See 'Visit the vet' in the chapter 'The first week'.

- Does the breeder have the relevant paperwork?

  The breeder must be able to give you a record of any vaccinations as this will need to be seen by the vet, as well as taken to any training classes or boarding kennels. They must also give you the relevant details if your puppy has been microchipped so you can change the contact details to your own.

A responsible breeder will:

- be happy to answer all your questions on the phone.
- ask questions of you to make sure their puppy is going to a good home.
- be happy to arrange a time for you to visit the puppies and their mother in the place where they were born and raised.
- be happy for you to have more than one visit before pick up if you feel you need it.
- provide genuine certificates or paperwork for vaccinations, microchipping, worming and results for health tests where relevant.
- be happy to send you more photos by phone or email if you feel you need them (especially if a visit means a lengthy journey on your part).

A responsible breeder will NOT:

- offer to deliver the puppy to you.
- offer to meet you at a random place.
- tell you the mother is out at the vets, or for any other reason. If she isn't there, the puppy most likely wasn't bred there, or there could be a problem with the mother.
- push you for payment.

Once you've found a litter of puppies you like, and you're sure they're healthy, happy and from a good home environment, set up your visit or visits.

Then find or buy a soft, comfortable blanket to take with you to your first visit. This is so that, if you do reserve a puppy, you can leave it with him until you pick him up. It will absorb the smells of mum and the litter mates until then, and help to make the separation less stressful.

Then the countdown begins …

Never get a puppy if you have any doubts about the seller or breeder.

3. TIME TO CHOOSE

When the day arrives you'll be eager to get going, but before you set off, remember to take that soft, comfy blanket to leave with the puppies in case you **do** decide to take one of them.

WHICH PUPPY?

The mother

It's well worth spending some time with mum. She must be friendly and good-natured if that is what you hope for in your puppy.

The owner/breeder

Try to make sense of the puppies' environment. Is it warm, friendly and homely? You want to be as sure as you can be that this is where they've grown up.

And if you were promised any paperwork on collection, you should ask to see it now.

The puppies

If you are absolutely sure you want a girl, it makes sense to ask the breeder to remove the boys while you meet the girls, or vice versa.

Chances are you've seen the photos and already have a firm favourite in mind. But don't rush this. Sit down with the puppies and spend all the time you need with them. Watch them playing, and see how they interact with you and their litter mates.

It's often said that you don't choose your dog or puppy, it chooses you. When we were choosing our current Jack Russell we were dead set on a tan-and-white female. And what did we get? A tri-coloured male. He chose us, then spent our entire visit convincing us he was the one we really wanted.

Basic checks

- Whichever one you choose, it should be happy, healthy, interactive, confident and curious.
- Check its teeth. Its upper and lower teeth should be in line, with the upper front teeth just over the lower front teeth.

- There must be no sign of mucus from the nose, bottom or genitals.
- The ears should be clean and not smelly.

Before you leave

In all likelihood, the breeder will ask for a deposit to secure your puppy.

Make sure too that you get a receipt and a written agreement that the contract is only binding if the puppy is in good health when you collect it.

Find out whatever you can about meals. What are the puppies being fed at the moment? How much and how often? Ask to see the food so you can be sure of giving him exactly what he is used to when you bring him home.

Finally, assuming you're coming back for the puppy at a later date, ask the breeder if you can leave that soft blanket with the litter. Then, when you pick him up, you will be able to bring all those familiar mummy-puppy smells with him into his new home.

4. PREPARING FOR THE BIG DAY

And now for everything you need to have in place before you pick up your bundle of joy and destruction. Buckets of love, oodles of patience and a fantastic sense of humour almost go without saying. And then there's all the paraphernalia ...

Things to buy, make or borrow

- **Soft blanket** – if you left this with the litter when you chose your puppy, be sure to collect it when you pick him up. Those familiar smells will help makes the transition far less stressful.

- **A crate** (also commonly referred to as a cage or den) – this will be your puppy's own space, a special place where he can be safe, quiet and keep his toys. There is more about this in the next three chapters, but for now choose one that is at least big enough for your puppy's basket or bed, toys and bowls – and for a full-grown Jack Russell to stand up, turn around and lie down in.

- **Comfortable bed** – this could be a basket or a dog cushion.

- **A collar or harness** – choose one that is soft, lightweight and comfortable. He will soon outgrow it and you can choose a sturdier one then if that's what you prefer.

- **A dog tag** – no need for cow bells. Choose one that is small and light and have it engraved with your name, address and contact number. (It's worth checking the legal requirements in your country or state.)
- **Short lead** (between three foot and six foot long) – again, nice and light. He's only tiny.
- **Bowls** – go for a non-tip design. Also consider a non-spill travel bowl for car trips, and a crate bowl that clips onto the door or side of your puppy's crate so that it can't be overturned.
- **Food** – start with the food your puppy has been served at his breeders. After that you can move him on to the food of your choice. If you are concerned about making the best decision, consult your vet at his first check-up.
- **Treats** – you will need lots of these. They are fantastic motivators when your puppy is first learning the rules, and just as good for reinforcing good behaviour. Choose treats that are suitable for puppies and avoid too many additives and preservatives, including sugar and salt. As a rule of thumb, the fewer ingredients the better.
- **A treat pouch** – a handy pocket for loose treats
- **Chews** – your puppy will spend around four hours of each day munching on things – at least until he's finished teething – so it's up to you to provide what you want him to do his chewing on. Chews make a fabulous alternative to table legs and leather shoes but, with a young puppy, avoid any chews that can splinter. Antler horns are good, and so are Kong toys filled with treats.

- **Toys** – can a puppy have too many? I think not. I suggest you invest in plenty of toys in all shapes, sizes, textures, colours and smells. He will chew on them, play with them and even snuggle up with them for hours.

- **Anti-chew or citronella** – it's worth investing in either of these to spray onto those things he absolutely must not chew on. Expensive chair legs for example.

- **Poo bags** – choose biodegradable to do your bit for the environment.

- **Wee mats/newspaper**

- **Carpet cleaner** – pet friendly

- **Odour eliminator** – pet friendly

- **Hot water bottle** – strong and covered

- **Grooming brush or glove** suited to his coat type

- **Pet carrier** – if he is likely to travel by car, please check the laws in your country as you might need to invest in a seat belt harness, pet carrier or dog guard.

The next things to do

- Arrange a date to pick up your puppy. Eight to nine weeks old is an acceptable time, but don't pick him up before he is eight weeks. If you are taking a car, it should be a day when at least one other person can accompany the driver.

- Book a visit to the vet for about two days after pick up.

- Puppy proof your home.
  - Secure the property. If you have a garden or yard,

ensure the borders are escape proof.

- ◦ If there is a pool, pond or any water he could fall into, fence it off.
- ◦ Check that there are no chemicals within reach (pesticides, weedkillers, fertilisers, etc).
- ◦ Cover or hide electricity cables and wires.
- ◦ Remove sharp objects and small things he could choke on.
- ◦ Be aware of any plants in your house and garden that may be poisonous. It's worth checking online for a comprehensive list, but these are some of the more common varieties: Aloe Vera, Ivy (Hedera Helix), Jade (Crassula Ovata), Hyacinth, Lily of the Valley, Asparagus Fern, Daffodils, Tulips, Azaleas, Crocuses, Foxgloves and Cyclamen.
- ◦ Keep valuables off the floor.
- ◦ Apply citronella or anti-chew to everything of great value that will be within his reach.
- • Choose a suitable place for the crate. It should be positioned against a wall in a room where he won't feel isolated – the room in your house that most of you spend most of the time in during the day.

Choosing a name

You could choose this once your puppy is home, but either way his name is more important than you might think. You will be using his name several times a day for years to come so it must be something he will easily recognise.

- • Animals respond better to shorter names – one-syllable names with a hard consonant or consonants like Duke or Zac for example, or two-syllable names such as Pop-py, Os-car or Til-ly. You might love the name Montgomery or Ophelia, but your dogs would thank you for calling them Monty or Oophy instead.

- Make sure the name you choose doesn't sound too much like a commonly-used command: No, Sit, Down, Stay, Come, Here, Good or Fetch. Beau and Jo, for example, sound too much like No.
- And don't choose a name that sounds like that of another member of the household. If your mother is called Anne, don't call puppy Dan; if your cat is Tigger, don't call puppy Digger or Trigger.
- Choose a name that is easy to call out. 'M' and 'n' sounds are soft which makes them more difficult to call out loudly than harder consonants like 'p', 't' and 'z'. Molly, say, is a less effective pet name than Pippy.
- Choose a name you are happy to call out loud in public.

5. PICKING UP YOUR PUPPY

'Happiness is
a warm puppy'

Charles M Schulz

The big day has finally arrived. If possible, pick him up early in the day so he can spend lots of time in his new environment before facing his first night without his mother and litter mates.

Remember, if you are driving, to make sure someone is with you to comfort and hold him.

Before you go

- If you haven't already set up his crate, set it up now and position it against a wall. Choose somewhere central – somewhere that he can feel safe, but without feeling isolated or excluded. Furnish it with the comfortable dog basket or bed, some toys, and also some treats if you like.

- And if you haven't already sprayed your most valued furniture with anti-chew, now's a good time.

Things to take

- The remainder of the payment (if necessary)
- An absorbent mat (or similar protection) in case he goes to the toilet in the car
- Poo bags and cleaning cloths
- Two bowls (one for food and one for water)
- A small amount of food (in a container)
- A bottle of water
- A small selection of toys and chews
- A backup soft blanket or cushion is also a good idea (in case something has happened to the one you left with the breeder)
- A collar or harness and your lead.

You're there

This is it! Give your new family member and best friend a gargantuan cuddle, have a play and check that he's still in good health:

- happy, confident and curious,
- that there are no signs of mucus from the nose, bottom or genitals,
- and that the ears are clean and not smelly.

Don't rush this.

In the excitement

Apart from your new and perfect puppy, you should come away with:

- the blanket you left, if you left one
- a note of his date of birth

- any relevant paperwork including a receipt of payment and the vaccination certificate. (And make sure you keep the breeder's full contact details in case of any questions.)
- information on the microchip, if he already has one. You will need the provider's details to register your puppy under your name and with its new address and contact details.

It's also worth double checking his food type (just in case it's been changed), and finding out what times he has been having his meals.

Thank the mother heartily for her beautiful puppy.

Travelling

Make sure your puppy is feeling safe and happy to be with you before you take him away for good. He is totally reliant on you now, so put yourself into those cute little paws that are being taken away from their mother and litter mates. Realise that he is leaving the only place he has ever known and, if you're driving, getting into a car for the first time too! Ask yourself, "How would I be feeling now?" and "What would I need from this new person or family?" You'd want to feel safe and secure, loved and cherished.

It's advisable to put on his collar or harness before you set off. This is best done with two people so one of you can hold and distract him while the other puts it on. If you're using a collar, you don't want it too tight or too loose. You should just be able to put two fingers between the collar and the puppy's neck. If you've brought a harness, you should also be able to fit two fingers (and no more) between your puppy and the harness at any point.

If you're travelling by car, and it is legal and safe, the passenger should hold him securely in the back seat. Later on your puppy can travel in his seat belt harness, pet carrier or dog guard, but for today being held is by far the kinder option. The passenger should keep him restrained – so the driver is not distracted – and love him and talk to him reassuringly. Your puppy will probably be too anxious for toys, but offer them anyway.

If the journey home is a long one, you'll need to attach the lead to his collar and stop every hour – more if you can – to give him a walk and the chance to go to the toilet. Keep him on the lead during breaks. He's unlikely to stray from you, but this would be a terrible place for him to get loose.

At every break, offer him some of the food and water in the bowls you've brought along. Like people, dogs can suffer from travel sickness, so it is possible he might be feeling a little ill or even be sick on the journey.

6. THE HOMECOMING

Give him a chance to wee before going inside.

Carry him into the house and put him near or in his crate, with the door wide open. Sit beside him, arrange the blanket smelling of his mother and the litter inside the crate, and give him a treat.

Then let him explore the crate and the house and stay by his side. If he doesn't venture to all areas of the house, give him a tour so that he knows all this is home.

All the treats today should be given in his crate. This will be his safe space and his very own bedroom. His comfy blanket should stay there and it is advisable to feed him there too. Do everything you can think of to make him feel that his crate is the best place in the world. If the crate design is very open, cover it with a blanket leaving gaps he can see out of.

Your puppy needs 18-22 hours' sleep a day at this age, and today he is likely to need even more than that. But your presence is essential for his peace of mind so, when you are sitting quietly, let him sit with you and sleep on your lap or close by.

Make sure there is always fresh water available to him, and that he knows where it is. And feed him what he is used to and, as far as practical, at the times he is used to. At this age he is most likely on four evenly-spaced meals a day. Aim to give him his last meal of the

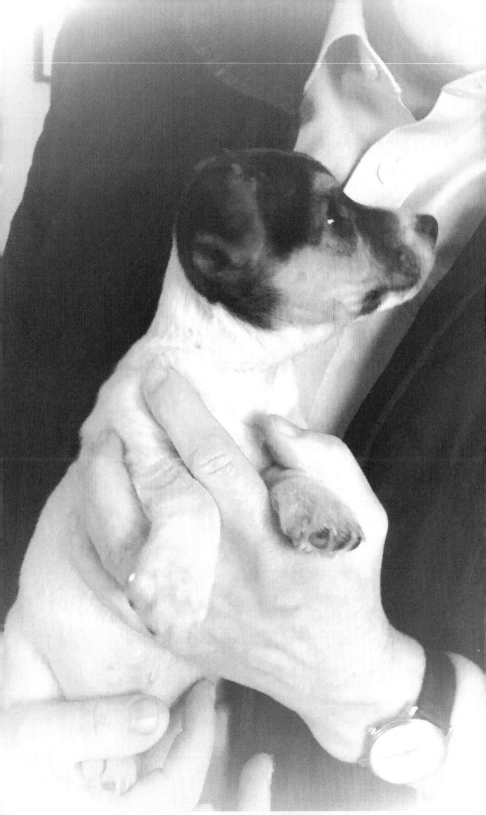

day a good two hours before his bedtime so he has a chance to go to the toilet.

At eight weeks puppies wee about once an hour and poop several times a day, so take him outside every hour if you can. He is still likely to piddle and poop in the house because he is so little, can't talk to you, and has no idea that doing this inside is a no-no. Toilet training is covered in more detail later on, but for now be sure to clean up after him very well, and use an odour eliminator.

Small children

If you have toddlers or young children, it is very important to supervise them when they are playing with your puppy. There is also more on this subject later in the book, when your puppy will have become more boisterous, but young children must understand NOW that your puppy is NOT a toy.

- They must not be allowed to pick him up.

- They must not be allowed to disturb him if he is sleeping or has taken himself to a quiet place.

- They must not run around squealing, and if the puppy becomes over-excited they should be calm and still.

- They should be allowed to play calm games, but nothing involving wrestling or tugging.

- They should always stay on their feet while playing with the puppy. If a child writhes on the ground with your puppy, he will treat it like a litter mate and mouth and bite.

Your other dogs

- Keep introductions short and sweet to start with, with your puppy on a lead to stop him from getting too close.

- If possible let them meet for the first time away from home. Choose somewhere your older dog has not been before because the excitement of the new environment will dilute the puppy's presence.

- Try to ensure the meeting place is somewhere no other dogs are likely to go (as your puppy is not protected by his vaccinations yet).

- Stand still or walk slowly when you let your puppy and your older dog meet, and don't interfere unless it becomes necessary.

- When you get home, if you have a garden, let the dogs meet there again, in the same way, before going inside. Let your puppy into the house first, before letting the older dog in.

- Lift any toys and food bowls off the floor for a few days.

- If you are worried about your puppy's safety, use a stair gate to separate the dogs in the short term, or put the puppy in its crate or a pen while the dogs get used to each other.

- Make sure all members of the family give the older dog more attention than usual.

Multiple dogs

If you already have more than one other dog, the process is the same but you should introduce the puppy to one dog at a time.

Cats

When your puppy is this young, it is unlikely to be a problem for your cat. Keep your puppy on a lead when they first meet, and have a lovely puppy treat at the ready. If your cat responds by hissing and spitting to begin with, your puppy will most likely retreat. But if the cat runs away, be ready to distract the puppy with the treat so he doesn't give chase. Always restrain him around the cat until he learns the cat is not something to be chased.

Always distract him with a toy or a game to teach him that playing with people is more fun than chasing the cat. It's debatable of course, but that's what we want him to think.

If you need to keep your puppy and the cat separated while you are out, use a stair gate or a puppy pen (a crate-like fence with sides but no top). Make sure the cat has safe places high up that it can reach instead of having to run away.

7. THE FIRST NIGHT

Uh-oh! Crunch time! He had his supper a couple of hours ago and it's time for bed!

- Take him outside for a last chance to go to the toilet. Stay with him in the place you'd most like him to go, and be patient.

- Back inside, make sure his crate is as appealing as possible, with his comfortable bed and his soft blanket.

Some people leave the crate in its place in the living area overnight, but considering the trauma to your puppy, and yourselves, there is a lot to be said for taking it to you room and placing it by the side of the bed. He still won't be able to snuggle up the way he's used to, but at least he can see you and hear you and knows he's not alone.

Open metal crates still leave your dog quite exposed. So if you've chosen one of these, put a blanket over all or part of it, making sure he can always see out of it.

It's a good idea to make a warm, but not too warm, hot water bottle, and wrap it carefully into his comfy blanket. This is to replicate the body warmth of his mother and litter mates when they snuggled up. Some people also put a ticking clock in the basket to mimic a heartbeat. And if the crate is not in your room, you could leave a radio playing softly to give him the sense he is not alone.

Scatter some toys and treats in the crate and make sure he has some clean water in his non-tip or clip-on bowl.

When crunch time comes, don't fuss over him. Just put him in the crate with a treat, as though he's the luckiest puppy in the world, and close the door.

In all likelihood he will cry at first, but he'll be warm, comfortable, fed and tired, so it shouldn't be for long.

If he is in your room, and you hear him shuffling around in the night, get up and take him outside to the toilet. He won't want to wee in his crate if he can help it. (And it won't be long before he doesn't need this break at all.)

If he's not in your room, you do need to get up early the next morning, and for the next few weeks at least, to take him outside.

8. KEEP OUT OF REACH!

Non-edibles

Your puppy will be chewing everything now, it's what puppies do best – either because they are teething or because they are using their mouths to find out about the world around them. But there are some non-edibles it's particularly important to keep out of reach:

- Medication – human medication is the biggest cause of pet poisoning.
- Toothpaste
- Pesticides
- Anti-freeze and other chemicals – many of these are sweet-tasting.
- A surprisingly high number of household and garden plants can be poisonous when eaten in large amounts. (Look up your specific plants on an up-to-date online list.)

Potentially poisonous foods

It's always best to feed your puppy or dog actual puppy or dog food, and simply stay clear of treats from your own plate. But there are some foods that you must never let him get hold of, never mind feed him, because, while they are perfectly safe for human consumption, they are potentially fatal to dogs. These include:

- Chocolate (especially dark chocolate)
- Xylitol (artificial sweetener, commonly used in sweets and gum)
- Alcohol
- Onion
- Garlic
- Grapes or raisins
- Avocado

Dangerous foods

- Soft bones, especially from chicken or pork, as they can get stuck in your dog's throat.

Also keep dogs away from

- Macadamia nuts
- Fruit pips or seeds
- Potato peels or green potatoes
- Rhubarb leaves
- Baker's yeast or yeast dough
- Broccoli
- Caffeine
- Mushrooms
- Persimmons
- Hops (generally in beer)
- Yeast dough

This is just a shortlist of some of the more common household foods and non-edibles you should keep away from your dog. It's not absolute and it's worth checking the most recently published data for a comprehensive list.

9. THE FIRST WEEK

From just three weeks old your puppy has been
socialising and learning to play with his mother and
litter mates. Now suddenly he must learn to be with
you, and with other people, and to figure out a whole
new set of rules. Luckily for you he is at his most
impressionable during these early days, so the time and
effort you put in now to building a positive relationship
will be worth buckets of good behaviour over the
months and years to come.

Your gorgeous bundle of innocence, mesmerisingly
cute as it is, needs a strong leader before it starts
walking all over you and making the decisions (as only
a Jack Russell can). And that leader needs to be you.
Starting now.

We will look at discipline and obedience training
later on but until you've read those, if he does
something you don't want him to do, don't punish him
or show aggression in any form. That would only
confuse him and make him fearful of you. Instead,
distract him and encourage him into doing something
else – something that is good. Then reward him for
listening. Encourage and reward – praise him at every
opportunity for the good things he does in your eyes, so
he can begin to learn what is right in your world. Be
clear and consistent in your praise and he will become
the most doting, loyal friend you could ever imagine.

Love him

Unconditionally. Do this and the rest will come naturally.

Teach him his name

Use his name to get his attention, and reward him when he responds to it. But be careful not to say the name over and over again or he will quickly become de-sensitised to it.

Make the crate appealing

Associations with the crate must be positive, so it should never be used for punishment.

- Make it comfortable and leave toys and treats inside so that it always feels welcoming and homely.
- If he has soiled in it, be sure to keep it clean.
- Encourage him into the crate and praise him when he goes inside.

Feed him

Your puppy should be having three to four meals a day at this stage. If you don't know how much to feed him, work out his daily allowance from the instructions on the food packaging. Split this allowance into three of four portions and work out a schedule for regular feeding, for example:

- Three feeds: 7am, 12.30pm and 6pm
- Four feeds: 7am, 11am, 3pm and 7pm.

  (Make sure the last meal of the day is a good two hours before bedtime so that he's less likely to mess in the house during the night.)

If he's on dry puppy food, you can add a little warm water and let it soak for a few minutes before feeding him. This makes it easier to eat and digest.

Fresh water should always be available.

TIP: Never let him get hold of anything listed in the previous chapter: 'Keep out of reach!'

Manage toilet time

Remember that your puppy is likely to need to wee every hour and poop several times a day. He just needs to learn when and where.

During the day, take him outside every hour if you can, and lead him to the spot you'd most like him to use. When he does it there, make sure he understands that was a good thing by making a HUGE fuss of him.

Give him a treat and tell him what a brilliant, amazing, spectacular dog he is.

At night, he won't want to go to the toilet in his crate but when he is very little he can only hold on for so long, so ideally you should get up during the night to take him out, as well as early each morning.

"But what about when he does mess inside?" you ask. What of it? He's a baby. Clean up well and be extremely patient. No matter what you've heard or read until now, don't punish him. He won't understand. (There's a whole chapter on toilet training coming up soon.)

Visit the vet

Regulations vary from place to place, but take his vaccination certificate with you and your vet will advise you on what your puppy needs and when. Most vaccines require several rounds, between six weeks and 16 weeks, so scheme these in during this first visit.

Be sure to tell the vet if you have plans to take your puppy to puppy classes or boarding kennels, because either of these require further inoculation.

If your puppy has not already been microchipped, it's advisable to have that done now too.

If his baby nails are very long and catching on everything, you could ask the vet or a veterinary nurse to clip them for you, or to show you how to do it yourself.

Make the visit fun for your puppy by giving him praise and attention, staying by his side when he gets his shots, and telling him how good he is. Possibly take him for a walk or give him a treat afterwards to create a positive association.

Handle him

Your puppy needs to learn that he is safe with people, that they mean him no harm, and that he has no reason to fear them or react defensively.

He should start learning this straight away, through lots of physical contact. Pet him and handle him: fondle his paws, move his legs, run your hand over his tail, feel his ears, touch his nose, gently examine his teeth, rub his tummy, groom him, pick him up and carry him around.

Play with him

Spend lots of time playing with him. And even now – in the post-vaccination days when he should stay inside your property – encourage him to experience the world through different surfaces. Put him on floor tiles, wood, carpet, grass, sand, rock, soft cushions, paper and blankets. Let him get used to them all.

Give him quiet time

He needs some time alone too so he can learn not to be anxious later on when you aren't there or able to play with him. Put him in his crate or a safe space for an hour, once or twice a day. If you have a garden or back yard, let him outside without you, or with just other dogs, for ten minutes every now and then.

Loosen his collar

Check the fit of his collar every few days. He is growing fast and it'll need to be loosened regularly. Remember that you should be able to fit two fingers between the collar and his neck.

10. FROM EIGHT TO ELEVEN WEEKS

FRAGILE! HANDLE WITH CARE!

Your puppy is weaning himself from his mother and you need to be ultra-sensitive to his feelings. Of course you should always be sensitive to his feelings, but this is the very worst time for anything to frighten him!

The time from eight to eleven weeks is known as the 'fear period'. It is a stage when he is over-sensitive and when negative stimuli are the most likely to leave a lasting impression. For example, a small child hurting him by pulling his tail or ears during this time could lead to a lifelong fear of small children.

This is also a time of opportunity. If he is already afraid of something, it is a good time to try to recondition him. For example, if he is afraid of umbrellas, show him that you are not afraid of them. Handle them gently in his presence without pressuring him in any way.

And from eight to eleven weeks is a particularly good time to show your puppy that most experiences are harmless. The more you expose him to the real world now, the less afraid he will be going forward.

The best way to help your puppy adjust to his new life in your world is to socialise him when he is still young. You will be able to teach him fancy dog tricks for years, but these next few weeks are the most important for getting him to socialise. Use them well and don't let them slip by.

Socialising means introducing him to as many people and animals of all shapes and sizes as possible. Visit friends and have friends to visit him. If puppy parties and puppy training are on offer in your area, take him along. (See the chapter 'Stepping out' for advice on meeting other dogs.)

HABITUATION

He should also be exposed to as many new places and conditions as possible. In all fairness, you can't shut him indoors then expect him to behave normally around new people, places and things.

Take your puppy with you everywhere you can and let him explore. Let him discover different smells, surfaces, sounds and sights. Take him into a park, to the school gates, for a walk along a river, go to a sports match, go to the shops. Walk him over and under bridges. Let him see cars and trucks and trains and planes. Thunder, lightning and snow might be hard to arrange, but ideally let him experience different weather conditions too. Take him out at night and in the rain.

Feeling safe

It is imperative though that during these new experiences he feels safe as well as having fun. Helping him to feel at ease in new situations is important for a happy and well-adjusted dog. Going forward, he can only be properly receptive to your training when he is feeling safe and confident, so stay with him through these new discoveries and don't let any of them frighten or over-excite him.

Here are some ideas to help with this.

- If you come across a potentially frightening situation – some big kids playing rough and tumble at the park for example – watch him closely for signs of discomfort. If he is hiding between your legs, or tucking his tail between his legs, you should back off and find a different route.

- Never put him under pressure to get close to anyone or anything.

- Be alert and sensitive to his feelings, so you will know when you can approach and when to stay away. There are many signs which mean different things in different contexts (see the chapter 'Puppy-People Translator').

- If you are not sure how he feels, avoid having a tight lead, so he knows he has a choice. If he is curious, approach from a distance. Let him look, listen and smell, gradually closing the distance as he is comfortable.

- You might want to pick him up and let him watch from your arms, but always be there for him as a reassuring presence.

Accidental noise

Don't forget about background noises that you are accustomed to, but might well frighten your puppy.

- TV and radio – Be especially alert during this time to sounds on TV or the radio. Dogs barking aggressively in a chase involving hounds, for example, could leave him terrified. Turn the sound down or off if he becomes alarmed – and before then if possible.

- Tension in the house – Keep a good vibe in the house. If he hears angry voices or senses a bad mood, he won't understand that it has nothing to do with him (whether it does or not).

- Fireworks – Close doors and windows, and muffle the sound with your own music or voices. Stay close to your puppy, showing him that you are not afraid.

BARKING

It is very important not to punish barking between eight and eleven weeks of age for all the reasons we've considered. Your puppy should be allowed to explore and to express himself.

If he is barking because he is afraid of something, and that fear is unfounded, lead him away from it and give him a treat. Reassure him with a gentle voice, then gradually expose him to whatever it is that he is afraid of, showing him that you are with him, that you are not afraid and that there is nothing to worry about.

AGGRESSION

Handling your puppy lots and often while he is very young is an excellent way to prevent him from developing aggressive behaviour later on. Teach him now that you can hold and touch him, his toys and his food whenever and however you please.

How?

By doing just that. Handle him, his toys and his food whenever and however you please. (Refer to the section on handling in the previous chapter.) That way he is less likely to become territorial and possessive over what he considers to be his things.

There is always a reason for aggression and it is usually founded on fear and insecurity. But whatever the cause, it is unacceptable towards you and others.

SMALL CHILDREN

It is widely accepted that having a dog as a cherished member of the family is good for children's emotional development. But small children need to be taught how to behave around your puppy, and they must be supervised when they play with him.

Many dogs, and small ones in particular, get snappy with children, and it's no wonder. Put yourself in their shoes and imagine being picked up continually, carried around, possibly even dropped, pestered, woken up. Imagine what it would be like not to be able to say, 'I don't want to play any more'. The only way your puppy or dog knows to tell someone they're hurting, tired, frightened or have had enough is to growl and snap. And the best way for you to manage this is to not make your puppy have to do this from the start.

The following points are reiterated from the chapter 'The homecoming' where we first talk about the importance of teaching small children that your puppy is NOT a toy.

- They should not be allowed to pick him up.
- They should not be allowed to disturb him if he is sleeping or has taken himself to a quiet place.
- They should not run around squealing, and if the puppy becomes over-excited they should be calm and still.
- They should be allowed to play calm games, but nothing involving wrestling or tugging.
- They should stay on their feet while playing, because if they writhe on the ground with the puppy, the puppy is likely to treat them like his litter mates and mouth and bite.

NOTE: If your puppy starts to growl menacingly at you or your child, call in a dog behavioural expert.

MOUTHING AND CHEWING

A lot of your puppy's nipping and biting is simply mouthing. He doesn't have hands so it's completely natural for him to play with you using his teeth. And if he is not play biting, he is probably chewing something, which is just as natural because he is teething. In time he will learn to control how hard he is biting and we will look at this in more depth in the chapter 'Mouthing and nipping'. In the meanwhile, keep an abundant supply of toys and treats at hand – lots of the things he IS allowed to chew on.

FURTHER CRATE TRAINING

If the crate started off at your bedside overnight, you should start to move it further from the bedroom – step by step if you like – to its permanent day-time position in the house. But only do this as your puppy grows in confidence and don't rush it. Your job is to build his trust.

If your puppy is going to be in the crate for a lengthy period while you are out, then you should leave him with some food as well as his water and toys.

FEEDING

When and how much

If you've been feeding your puppy four times a day, then by nine or ten weeks (or when you sense he is ready) you can cut this back to three times a day. Divide his daily food allowance (according to the instructions on the pack) into three portions instead of four and alter your schedule for regular feeding to, for example, 7am, 12.30pm and 6pm. Avoid feeding too close to your bedtime, so he's less likely to mess in the house or his crate during the night.

Change of food

If you are changing your puppy's food, incorporate the new brand slowly to avoid digestive problems and help him to adjust to the new taste. For example, for two to three days give him one quarter of the daily allowance of the new food with three quarters of the daily allowance of the old. A few days later make it half of one and half the other, again for a few days, increasing the new food to three quarters and finally moving fully over to the new food.

Reminders

- Don't give your puppy scraps from the table.
- Don't let him con you into giving him more food than his daily allowance.
- Don't let him get hold of anything listed in the chapter 'What NOT to give your puppy'.

COLLAR

Check that his collar is not getting too tight. He is growing fast and it'll need to be loosened regularly. Remember, you should be able to insert two fingers between the collar and his neck.

GROOMING

Brushing

Jack Russells don't usually shed a lot of hair, but they still need regular brushing, even if your puppy has a short coat. Use a dog brush or grooming glove suited to his coat type, and groom him every two to three days. This is also very good for teaching your dog to be handled, especially during vet visits.

Washing

Avoid bathing your young puppy because his natural oils are keeping his skin and coat healthy.

If he really does need washing, try to keep baths to no more than one a month. Use a quality dog shampoo, have towels at the ready and wear old clothes. Ease him into an empty bath or washtub, offering lots of praise and treats. Run the water luke warm before soaking him with a wet sponge. Rub in the shampoo and lather, then rinse several times, working the shampoo out with your hands. Bathe his head last because this is when he will shake the most. Wrap him in a towel and rub him down thoroughly. Use a hair dryer if you like but NEVER on a hot setting – always cool or warm, and test it on yourself first.

Nails

Your dog needs his nails, but if they are unmanageably long they will need clipping. Perhaps you had this done at his first vet visit, but if not, and you feel confident enough to do it yourself, you can buy your own clippers. With your dog standing up, pick up a foot so it bends naturally.

Holding it in your empty hand, look for the part of the nail you can see through if you hold a light to his paw. You want to avoid the 'quick', which is inside the nail and contains sensitive nerve endings. Jack Russells often have a combination of white and black nails. The whiter the nails, the easier to see the quick. If the nails are dark, clip a tiny bit at a time, then inspect to make sure there is no bleeding. You can file them smooth with an emery board.

Teeth

There are lots of treats on the market that double as dental chews to clean your puppy's teeth and keep his gums healthy.

If you want to clean his teeth and to clean them by brushing, you can buy dog toothbrushes and meat-flavoured pastes.

TIME ALONE

The best way to prevent separation anxiety at a later stage is to start leaving your puppy on his own occasionally during the day. If he is lucky enough to be right by your side for most of the time this is even more important.

- Choose a time when he is getting tired and likely to sleep soon.
- Take him outside for a little play and a toilet break.
- Shut him in his crate with everything he needs (or put him in his bed and shut him in the room).
- Ignore any whining and leave the room or go out for a short while.

- If he is asleep when you return, open the crate door so he can get out when he wakes.

- Start off with about ten minutes and build it up slowly to no more than an hour at this stage. For one thing, he will be needing the toilet.

TRAINING

This is about mutual understanding, communication and a better life for your puppy as well as everyone else in the family. Training isn't something you merely practice at obedience classes or from time to time. It starts the minute your puppy enters your life and is an ongoing, moment-by-moment process. And every member of the family and household should be involved, using the same set of rules, spoken commands and body language.

The upcoming chapters 'Behaviour' and 'Training' cover the key dos and don'ts to help you build a strong foundation for a relationship with your puppy based on understanding and respect.

PLAYTIME

Don't just put your puppy outside with his toys. Play is social interaction so you, or a member of the family, needs to actually play with him.

Play is so important that there's a separate chapter ('Playtime!') with key pointers to help you make every game and every playtime a positive experience. The chapter also has ideas for toys and games, and you will soon figure out his favourites as well as the ones you play best together.

EXERCISE

All dogs need exercise so they don't get bored, unruly, overweight or unhealthy. Your full-grown Jack Russell will need half an hour to two hours of exercise a day, but between eight and eleven weeks of age take your puppy on walks of no more than 10-15 minutes a time. As a rough guide, add five minutes to the length of each walk per month, so that by four months, he should ideally have two walks a day of approximately 20 minutes each. The chapter 'Stepping out' has lots more advice and tips for your outings.

Once you start taking him out you might want to invest in a harness (if you haven't already) and/or an extendable lead:

- **A harness** – the advantage of a harness is that it puts no pressure on your puppy's throat when he is learning to walk on the lead. This should be a suitable size, adjustable, and comfortable.

- **Extendable lead** – used carefully, and only once your puppy is used to the short lead, an extendable lead can make walks more enjoyable for you and your puppy because the longer rein gives him more freedom. BUT an extendable lead also means you have less control so it's worth noting here that they can be dangerous:

  - for him (he might run into the road),

  - yourself (you might get caught up in it if he dashes after something),

  - and also for nesting birds and small animals (which could be hiding just off the path).

As a result they are not always permitted in parks and conservation areas.

NOTE: Puppies grow up fast compared with human children. One week in your puppy's life is equivalent to around five months' development in a human child.

11. TWELVE WEEKS PLUS

Although at twelve weeks your puppy is still heavily dependent on you, and ever so eager to please, he will start leaving your side to explore more. You will still be on his radar all the time but, on the bright side, you will stop tripping over him whenever you step backwards.

His socialisation is still incredibly important and should be ongoing.

As for chewing, he will be munching on everything.

TEETHING

By twelve weeks, your puppy's adult teeth, a full 42 of them, are waiting to push out those super-sharp baby teeth. It then takes until around 18 weeks for those baby teeth to even start falling out. That's a lot of weeks of important chewing to be done so – for the sake of your puppy, your house and your sanity – always have an abundant and ready supply of toys and treats he is allowed to chew.

We will look at chewing again under 'Discipline'.

SLEEP

By twelve weeks, your puppy no longer needs the 18-22 hours' sleep he needed when you brought him home, but he does still need around 16 hours of sleep or rest a day.

The following chapters (up until 'Puppy-People Translator') focus on specific aspects of behaviour, training and care – the most important and pressing puppy issues – and are filled with useful tips to help you as you guide your puppy into adolescence and beyond.

TIP: When your puppy becomes over-excited, a good way to calm him down is to tickle him on the sides of his face just under his ears, while lulling him with soothing words like 'Settle' or 'Calm down'.

12. BEHAVIOUR

Your puppy loves you so much! He wants to learn from you and please you. But he only knows what his survival instincts tell him so, to reiterate, it's your job to teach him what is and isn't allowed in your world. We will look at specific behaviours in the next chapters, but the pointers in this general chapter are fundamental to all of these and will help you to make better sense of them too.

For a well-behaved puppy, the first thing to understand – as you surely do by now – is that puppies are much more receptive when they have nothing to fear. A fearful puppy will never be totally engaged. Our understanding of animal behaviour is improving all the time, and it's no longer acceptable to punish dogs, never mind puppies, by shouting, smacking and rubbing their noses in the carpet. This sort of treatment is both ineffective and counter-productive. It scares your puppy and puts you in a bad mood. You lose your dog's trust and the spinout of that – into all the other areas of the relationship – is just not worth thinking about. You want your puppy to be happy and optimistic, looking forward to everything, rather than fearing it.

So how do you achieve this? In a nutshell: you gain his trust by focusing on the things he does right. By encouraging good behaviour and rewarding it!

Encourage and reward

Always tell him what you DO want him to do, rather than what you DON'T want him to do. Let's say for example he's got the TV remote between his teeth. Don't shout and get angry! Calmly distract him with something else, something he IS allowed to chew on. Refocus him on this new and exciting toy, and rescue the remote. If you don't have anything at hand, then ask him to do something to obey you – even something as simple as a 'Sit!' once he can do that.

His feelings are everything

Let's say your puppy bounds up to you with glint in his eye, a wag in his tail and a captured, disheveled bath mat in his mouth. Try not to think about your favourite bath mat which, after all, is just a thing and has no

feelings at all! Instead, think about HOW HE'S FEELING about what he's done. He thinks he's done brilliantly, doesn't he? He wants a medal. Scold him now and you'll really confuse him. Then again, if you praise him, he might keep bringing you bath mat-type presents ad infinitum. So what do you do?

You don't scold or praise. Distract him instead by calling him to you and getting his attention onto something else, a toy perhaps. When he is refocused on the toy, offer him a tempting chew. By then the bath mat should be far from his mind, and you should be able to rescue it. And if it's still functional, remember to hang it up out of his puppy-jaw reach.

You are the leader

To establish a positive relationship, your puppy must understand from the start that, even though you love him and you are best friends, your word is law and he must listen to you. And he will, as long as you are a worthy leader and a good teacher. Here are some key tips for you.

- Don't be aggressive towards him. Instead, be gentle but firm.

- Don't go too easy on him either. In the long run that can be as unfair as punishing him.

- Be crystal clear in your instructions. Use single-words rather than sentences and try to be consistent in your choice of words. Don't switch between 'Come!' and 'Here!' for example, or 'Walk!' and 'Heel!'.

- Keep your tone positive.

- Use body language as well as verbal commands.

- When he does what you want, show him unreservedly how clever he is. Be happy and excited, and reward him with praise.

Timing is all-important

It's vital that you teach your puppy with timely signals – signals that apply to what he is doing AT THAT TIME. If you discipline him for something he did two minutes ago, he won't understand the reason. For example, if he runs off after a cat and then comes back, and you shout at him for chasing the cat as he is coming back, he will naturally think you are shouting at him for coming back and not for chasing the cat. The result? He is confused and intimidated, and next time he will think twice about coming back. Too many well-meaning dog owners make the mistake of misplaced timing – and it's terribly unfair.

Rules must be consistent

If one person lets your puppy onto the sofa, it's downright unfair for someone else to reprimand him for being there. Rules will be very confusing if they differ from person to person, so it's really important that everyone in your puppy's life understands and teaches what is and what isn't allowed in precisely the same way.

Prevent bad behaviour

- Make sure your puppy's basic needs are met: food, water, warmth, things to chew on, sleep, play, exercise and exploration. If he has all of these he is far less likely to behave badly in the first place.
- Don't put temptation in his way. If you don't want

him eating from your dinner plate, don't leave it lying around, unattended and in easy reach. That's just setting him up to fail.

- And try to anticipate things that might go wrong. Table cloths, for example are begging for trouble. Don't use them until he's older. And if you think he's about to chase the cat, hold on to him and distract him with a toy.

Let him know when you disapprove

In many bad behaviours, the best way to tell a Jack Russell you don't like what he's doing is to take away something he wants – your attention. Discourage bad behaviour by ignoring him when he is behaving in any way that is not acceptable to you. Stop play, walk away, look away, leave the room if you can.

When to say 'No!' or 'Leave!'

1. When your puppy does something totally unacceptable.
2. When he boldly ignores your voice command because he would rather do something else.

These need to be corrected immediately and here's how.

- Reprimand him straight away. Say 'NO!' or 'LEAVE!' in a voice that is loud and startling enough to prevent or stop his behaviour. It should be in stark contrast to your usual quiet and calm voice, and used sparingly for best effect.
- Block his way with your body, or physically stop him if you need to.
- Then make eye contact and use your voice to get him to focus on you.

- Once you have his attention, praise him for changing his focus.

- The trouble with 'No' and 'Leave' is that your puppy doesn't know what he's meant to do instead. Always try to give him something better to do or to chew on.

Still struggling?

If you've tried all these things with a bad behaviour, with clear and consistent communication, and you're still struggling, you can resort to time-out. Shut him in the kitchen, or similar safe place, and leave him for a few minutes – five is acceptable, ten is too long.

Alternatively you can tie him up in a safe and suitable time-out spot, and ignore him for five minutes. The lead should be just long enough for him to be able to sit up and lie down comfortably.

Serious behavioural problems

If your puppy develops any serious behavioural traits – for example ones that could endanger you, himself, or any other person or their dog – you should get help from a professional in dog behaviour.

Let's look at some common problem behaviours in more detail.

13. JUMPING UP

Your puppy will jump up because he is happy to see you, because he loves you, because he wants you to pet him and play with him. Although he is used to jumping up on his mother and litter mates, he now needs to learn not to jump up on you or other people. You might not mind his jumping now – after all Jack Russells are small dogs, and not likely to bowl anyone over with their loving greetings – but other people might mind, especially when he has muddy little paws or sharp claws, so you want to nip it in the bud before it gets out of hand.

Do not
- Reward him for jumping up
- Tell him to get down
- Talk to him
- Push him away
- Shout or yell
- Smack him or use physical punishment of any sort.

Do
- Look away from him
- Turn away from him
- Lift your hands away and don't touch him

- After a few seconds, come back, and repeat if necessary
- When he has quietened down and stopped jumping, be sure to praise him and reward him.
- Get all family members to do this, and ask visitors to help with this too.
- If jumping up on visitors is likely, put him on a lead before opening the door.

How does it work?

It teaches him that if he jumps up he will get no attention, and that if he keeps his four paws on the ground he will be praised.

14. TOILET TRAINING

Your puppy needs to wee about once an hour and poop several times a day. He doesn't know that inside the house is a no-no. This is something he needs to learn and it will take time and patience.

In a nutshell: When he goes to the toilet outside, and as soon as he has finished, it's party time. Reward! Reward! Reward! That way you will teach him that doing his business outside means AMAZING things will happen.

Here are some key Dos and Don'ts to speed up the process.

Do

- When your puppy arrives at your house for the first time, give him a guided tour. The sooner he understands that all this space is living area, the sooner he will stop using it as a toilet.

- Take him outside every hour.

- Take him outside immediately if you spot any of these tell-tale signs:
  - Sniffing and circling the floor
  - Whining
  - Pacing up and down
  - Scratching the floor.
- Lead him to the spot you'd like to encourage him to use.
- Then wait. And wait some more. Stay out there with him – come rain or shine – watching him all the time.
- You can spur him on with an encouraging command, like 'quickly now' or 'wee time'.
- Wait until he's completely finished before you reward him, or he might only do half his business.
- As soon as he is finished, shower him with praise.
- When he goes to the toilet inside, thoroughly clean the place he's marked and use a pet-safe odour eliminator. Your puppy is most likely to go to the toilet somewhere he can already smell wee or poop. So the best way is to teach him where to make his messes is to keep your house clean. (If possible, limit your puppy's access to carpeted areas.)
- If he has messed inside but on a training mat or piece of newspaper, then carry this outside to where you would like him to go instead, and weigh it down there. The smell will act as a signal to him to do his business there.

Do not

- Don't punish him for piddling or pooping inside. Punishing him for something he can't help and doesn't fully understand will make him nervous and slow his progress.
- Don't leave him outside on his own. He will just turn his attention to getting back to you, and when he does get back inside the house he will very likely still need to go.

How does it work?

It teaches him that if he goes to the toilet in certain acceptable places then he is being a very good puppy and will be showered with love and attention.

How long will toilet training take?

Progress varies from puppy to puppy but it can up to six months. Be patient.

TIP: Once your puppy understands that you want him to do his toiletries outside, you can hang a bell on a string from the door that leads to outside. He might well learn to jingle the bell to tell you when he needs to go out.

- **FYI** - Your puppy will never wee or poop to spite you.
- **FYI** - Some dogs will make a little wee as a sign of submission, some will wee with excitement. These should never be punished.

15. MOUTHING AND NIPPING

All dogs love to play, and play involves mouthing each other, so it's completely natural for your puppy to want to play bite. He might also bite because he is teething. If, like many new puppy owners, you don't mind your puppy chewing your hands now, you soon will. As he gets older, the biting will get harder and involve others too, so he should learn as soon as possible not to use his teeth on people.

Adult dogs are good at controlling the pressure of their jaws but puppies often make the mistake of biting too hard because they are still learning and practising jaw control. If a puppy bites one of its litter mates too hard while playing, the hurt puppy will yelp and stop playing. Your puppy has already learned from the other puppies that biting too hard inhibits play time.

He will learn gradually to play more gently until he understands not to let his teeth into contact with your skin at all.

Do

- Play with him with a chew toy in your hand. If he bites you and inflicts pain, make a high yelping sound and immediately withdraw your hand. This is exactly what would have happened with his litter mates, so it will help him to learn that it's okay to nip the chew toy, but not your hand.

- If the biting persists, remove yourself from the game, the room even, just for a few minutes to show him that teeth on skin equals no more playing. It's not a quick fix, but he will gradually make the association.

- Supervise small children. Their tendency when a puppy mouths them is to scream and run around, which only excites the puppy even more.

Do not

- Don't shout at him or smack him if he mouths or nips. This can make the biting harder to control.

- Don't rush him. He must learn jaw control gradually and through experience.

- Cut back on playing rough tug games which just encourage biting.

How does this work?

It teaches him that if his teeth make contact with your skin, you will stop playing with him. And if they don't, the fun and games are more likely to continue.

16. CHEWING HOUSE AND HOME

*'Puppies are constantly inventing new ways to be
bad. It's fascinating. You come into a room they've
been in and see pieces of debris and try to figure out
what you had that was made from wicker or what
had been stuffed with fluff'*

Julie Klam

All dogs chew, especially puppies! They chew things
either because they are teething or simply to explore.
Chewing is how they learn about the world around
them. They don't have hands, so they inspect
everything they can with their mouths and teeth.

Your puppy will chew on anything he can, so it's
really important to give him things you are happy for
him to chew on.

Do not

- Leave valuable chewables, like shoes, lying around
  on the floor. Puppies are excellent training for
  untidy owners.

- If you find your puppy chewing something he
  shouldn't, don't try to take it away from him, and
  especially don't start a tug-of-war.

- Don't give him sticks. They can splinter and get
  stuck in his mouth.

Do

- Instead, give him something he is allowed to chew on.

- Buy lots of puppy toys and treats. Pet toys are created to appeal to your dog by smell, taste, feel and shape, but you can also use old soft toys.

- Keep these prizes close by; you never know when you'll be needing them.

- When your puppy chews something he shouldn't, replace it with something he can and should. Make sure your replacement offering is a toy you know he loves. As he plays with the forbidden item, hold the preferred toy to his nose and say, 'Leave!' or 'Drop!'

- When he drops it, you can give him the treat and a pat.

- If you see him approaching something with demolition on his mind, call him with a happy voice. Puppies are easily distracted and he should immediately forget what he'd planned to do and come running to you. Reward him for coming and give him something more suitable to get his teeth into.

- If your puppy's got a taste for something that can't be moved – a table leg for example, spray it with a pet-friendly anti-chew, or citronella.

TIP: Tie a knot in an old sock and give it to him as a toy. He'll think Christmas has come early.

How does all this work?

It helps to protect your sanity, precious personal items and objects of value. And to keep him happy and out of mischief.

17. BARKING

Yapping at you

As your puppy comes to see that efforts to win your attention, like jumping up or nipping, are fruitless, he might well replace these with his latest greatest trick – an unpleasantly ear-piercing yap which says:

- I am still here you know.
- Stop ignoring me.
- Hey, I want some of that too.
- Let's play.
- Pick me up …
- … or any of the above.

  Whatever it is, he wants your attention.

Don't

- Don't give it to him.

Do

  Instead pull out your best ignoring him techniques:

- Look away from him
- Turn away from him
- Don't talk to him
- Lift your hands away and don't touch him

- Leave the room if you can
- When he has quietened down, be sure to acknowledge and reward him.

Barking at 'intruders'

It's natural for your Jack Russell to alert you to what he considers to be intruders, and also to bark at passers by, and that kind of barking is not necessarily something you want to stop or even discourage.

But if your puppy is barking at a passer by – or the neighbour's cat, which is more likely at this stage – and you do want him to stop, your instinct is probably to shout at him to keep quiet. But put yourself in his shoes and you will see that if you shout at him while he is barking, he will just think you are egging him on, or even coming to help. The result? He will bark even harder.

So with unwanted yapping or barking, as with pretty much all bad behaviour, it is more effective to distract him or just give him the 'I'm ignoring you now!' treatment.

18. DIGGING

It's absolutely natural for Jack Russells to dig. That's not to say your puppy will, because not all Jack Russells do. But if your puppy does take too much of a liking to digging, here's what to do.

- Find him a place where he IS allowed to dig.
- Bury things for him in that spot and let him find them.
- Then, if you find him digging in other places, tell him 'No!' or 'Leave!', fill the hole he has made back up, and show him where he can and should dig instead.

TIP: If the problem persists, make an unpleasant clanging noise whenever you see him starting to dig. Hit a pot with a metal spoon for example. Soon he'll associate digging – either in that place or altogether – with this horrible noise.

19. STEPPING OUT

Once your puppy has been fully vaccinated you can start walking him out and taking him on outings. But first he needs to practise walking on the lead at home and, while you're waiting for his vaccinations to take effect is the ideal time.

Eventually you want him walking by your side on a loose lead, but for a puppy, with seemingly endless stores of pent-up energy, this is surprisingly difficult to learn.

Do

- Use a normal collar and short lead. No choke chains.
- Attach the lead when he is calm and not resisting you.
- Start by letting him wander around the house with the lead trailing behind him, but try not to let him chew it.
- The next stage is to pick up the lead and encourage him to walk along beside you.
- If he pulls, stand still and call him to you. Praise him, then try again.
- When he is walking nicely alongside you, with the lead slack but off the ground, reward him generously with praise and treats.

Don't

- Use a choke chain or half check.
- Don't drag him. That would only make him panic and pull away.
- Don't be pulled along by him. That would teach him that pulling works in his favour.
- If he is pulling, don't pull back, or yank on the lead, or shout at him. Instead, call him to you and praise him for coming.

When the time comes for him to get out and about, here are a few things to consider and be aware of.

Safety

Think carefully about where you're going to take him so you can avoid frightening or stressful experiences.

- Choose a safe, open space away from busy roads.
- A place where other dog owners are likely to act in a responsible way.
- And think about the best time to go. Perhaps it's too soon for a Saturday morning at the park if there is likely to be a noisy football match in play?

If something does scare him on an outing, let him know you are with him, protecting him and that he is safe.

What to take:

Make sure you have him on his lead (a short one is better to start with) and are armed with:

- Poo bags – more than one
- Treats (ideally in a treat pouch) – so you can reward good behaviour

- Water and a bowl – if there is no clean water where you are going.

Pooping

If he poops, pick it up.

Other dogs

When you come across other dogs on your outings, you could use the opportunity for your puppy to practise the meeting and greeting we introduced in the section on 'Socialisation'. But never assume that other people or their dogs are happy to reciprocate. And never let your dog run up to other dogs unless their walkers have told you it's okay. There are lots of reasons why it might not be. Perhaps the dog is very old; maybe it is injured; or not good with puppies; or the owner is working on a specific training exercise. Always ask first and from a distance:

1. whether their dog is good with puppies and
2. whether they are happy for your puppy to say 'hello'.

If it is okay for your dogs to meet, stay close by to supervise, and to pre-empt any bad experiences.

- Make sure you walk past some dogs, and people too, so your puppy doesn't take it for granted he can run up to anyone for a chin- and tail-wag.

Play dates

- If your puppy meets another dog he plays well with, you could arrange play dates at times that suit you both.

Together time

- Put your smart phone out of temptation's way and make this quality time with your puppy!

- If you are going somewhere with big open spaces like the park, you can take a lead with a long line. But NEVER pull your puppy back with the line. He should come to you as called. There is more on this in 'Training'.

20. TRAINING

"Properly trained, a man
can be dog's best friend"
Corey Ford

It's normal to assume that puppy training is about training your puppy – most people do – but in actual fact it is nearly all about you, the owner, learning how to communicate effectively with your puppy.

And puppy training is not about tricks either. It is about basic obedience to improve communication and understanding. It is all about a better quality of life for you, your puppy … and everyone he meets.

Everything from the chapter on Behaviour applies to this chapter too because the premise for training is the same. Because your puppy is more engaged when he has nothing to fear, train by encouraging and rewarding good behaviour. Always tell him what we DO want him to do, rather than what we DON'T want him to do.

When to start

Training starts the moment your Jack Russell enters your life. Even if you've signed up for puppy classes at some future date. Don't wait. Just teach him little by little, moment by moment. Practice often, and never give up.

94

Who's responsible?

Anyone and everyone in your puppy's close and extended family. Commands will be very confusing if they differ from person to person, so it's really important that everyone involved in training your puppy uses the same spoken commands, hand signals, body language and rules.

Where

Start training in a quiet place with no outside distractions. A closed room is infinitely better than a park with other puppies play-fighting nearby.

NAME RECOGNITION

One of the first things your puppy should learn is to recognise his name. After all, how else will he know that you're communicating with him?

Do

- From a short distance – one or two metres is fine – call your puppy clearly, using his name just once.
- Use a happy, friendly voice.
- Crouch down if you can.
- Open your arms to welcome him (body language is important).
- Make a fuss of him when he gets to you.
- If he doesn't respond, wait a few seconds then call again, still clearly, and still just the once.
- When he does come, praise him lovingly, give him a small treat and tell him how brilliantly clever he is.
- Practise this often.

Don't

- Don't overuse his name or say it repeatedly in quick succession, or he will soon learn to ignore it.

EYE CONTACT

If your puppy is not looking at you, he is probably not listening either. Calling his name will encourage him to look at you and, when he does, you can know he's engaged. He's turning to you to find out what's coming next: will you open the door, take him for a walk, throw the ball? It is excellent that he is turning to you for answers and provision, so make sure you reward him.

CALLING HIM TO YOU

This is important for your relationship, and essential for your puppy's safety. It is much like the name recognition exercise.

Now, when he is little, is a very good time to teach him recall because he needs you more than ever for love, food and safety. Chances are he is with you right now, under your feet or helping you to absorb this book. Digest it even.

Do

- Follow the steps in the Name Recognition exercise above, using his name and adding a word like "Come!" or "Here". Consistency is key, so choose which word you prefer and stick with it.
- Call him to you regularly.
- Practice at home on a lead before you let him go when you are out and about.
- When you do let him off the lead away from home, make sure it is in a very safe place.
- Practice letting him go and calling him back.

Don't

- Punish him if he doesn't come straight away. He will think he's being punished for coming to you, and will think twice the next time about coming back at all. (See 'Timing is all-important' in the chapter on Behaviour.)
- Don't always put him back on a lead when he comes to you, or he will soon learn that coming means the end of his free-play session. Only put him back on the lead after several recalls.

'SITTING'

A reliable 'Sit' is one of the most useful exercises you can teach your puppy.

- Call your puppy to you and hold a treat, palm facing down, just in front of his nose for him to smell.

- When you've got his interest, slowly take the treat up a couple of inches and over his head.

- When he lowers his bottom, say "Sit!" and give him the treat.

- When he is doing this well, move on to the next stage. Wait until his bottom is actually on the floor before you say "Sit!", and then only give him the treat.

- He will soon learn to associate the word with the action. In time you can teach him to sit for longer stretches, from further away and during distractions.

LYING 'DOWN'

- It is best to start teaching this command when your puppy is already in an attentive sit.
- Without feeding him the treat in your hand, move your hand, still palm down, from above his nose and towards the floor, between his front paws and close to his body.
- When he lowers his nose and front paws, keeping his bottom on the ground, say "Down!" in a clear voice and give him the treat.
- When he is doing this well, you can wait until his tummy and all four paws are on the floor before you say "Down!", and then only give him the treat.

WALKING ON THE LEAD ('HEEL')

If your puppy is not yet used to walking on the lead, practise this at home first. (See the previous chapter 'Stepping out'.)

Basic training

There are lots of other useful commands your puppy can learn including:

'Stand'
'Off' or 'Leave'
'Stay'
'Settle down'
'Heel'.

There are some excellent obedience training books on the market if you'd like to add to these basics, and if training classes are available in your area, they are well worth the time and effort, and your dog would love them too.

Extension exercises

- **Duration** – Once your puppy can do an exercise, like 'Sit' for example, you can gradually get him to sit for longer periods before treating him.

- **Distractions** – You can slowly increase the distractions too. A 'Sit' when a squirrel is taunting him from a nearby tree is very different from a 'sit' in a quiet place. Once he's mastered the instruction in a quiet room, start practising it in a busier part of the house, then on a street corner, then at the park, and so on.

- **Distance** – In time, you can also begin asking your puppy to 'sit' from slightly further away from you, like the other side of the room.

What if the training's not working?

If your puppy doesn't do what you've asked (assuming he's not hard of hearing):

- he doesn't understand and needs clearer instructions,

- he needs more practice,

- or he needs a better reason to obey you – like a treat, an even better treat, or higher praise.

TIP: Your voice and treats are key to training your puppy, but don't forget about gestures. Most dogs respond better to body language than to words.

21. PLAYTIME!

Playing with your puppy helps to develop his social skills, improve his communication skills, and gives him the mental and physical exercise Jack Russells so badly need.

But most importantly of all, it's great fun.

GAMES

These are some games you can try. All puppies have their favourites and you will soon figure out which ones you play best together.

Treasure hunt

He'll love this. It is basically rooting around for hidden treasure.

1. Make sure he can't see you, then hide treats and toys in the garden for him to find.
2. Take him into the garden with you and encourage him to find and follow your scent. The first few times you might need to guide him.

Which hand?

1. With your hands behind your back, put a small treat or two in one hand and nothing in the other.
2. Make your hands into fists and bring them in front of you.
3. Let your puppy choose which fist he prefers the smell of.
4. When he's decided which hand he's interested in, and it's the right one, say 'Good!' and open your hand, letting him take the treat.

Chase

This game is excellent practice for encouraging your puppy to come to you when he is older.

1. Flick a treat across the floor.
2. Let him chase after it.
3. When he comes back for more, make eye contact and praise him.
4. Then flick another treat across the floor, and so on.

Fetch

This is like chase, but outside or in a much bigger space.

1. Throw things for him to fetch: toys, a ball, a treat.
2. Say 'fetch' as you throw each item.
3. Once he knows to 'fetch', start throwing the objects into harder-to-reach places.
4. If this doesn't work, throw more interesting toys or tastier treats.

Obstacle course

1. Turn your passageway or garden into an obstacle course – build jumps, make tunnels, fill a tea tray with a centimetre of water, arrange boxes to navigate around … anything you can think of that is safe.
2. Guide your puppy through the course and reward him with treats each time he overcomes an obstacle.

TOYS

To keep your puppy interested in his toys, don't put them all out at the same time. Only let him play with or chew a couple at a time, and rotate them during the day or through the week.

The Maze

- There are a number of 'slow feeder' pet toys on the market which are maze-like in design. They are intended for dogs who gulp their food down too fast, but they also work brilliantly for brain-training.
- Put a treat or two in the middle and let him use his paws, snout and tongue to work the treats out of the maze before he can eat them.

The Kong

- This is a hard, hollowed rubber toy that is available online and from most pet stores. Fill it with Kong treats or other small treats, or fill it with marmite or peanut butter (make sure it contains no Xylitol). Your dog will spend hours trying to crunch or lick it out.

Activity balls

- There are plenty of these on the market in a range of shapes and sizes. Put dry food or treats inside one of these and your puppy will love rolling it around to get the pieces out.

THE RULES OF PLAY

1. Several short play sessions spread throughout the day are better than one long one.

2. Start playtimes when your puppy's being good, so you're not rewarding him for bad behaviour.

3. Whatever games you're playing, remember he's only little, so don't overpower him. Be sure to match your strength, speed and energy to his own.

4. As far as possible, get down low to his level (small children excepted).

5. If a toy is involved, avoid hard tugging. Never let his feet leave the ground as he clings to a toy. It puts too much pressure on his teeth, and encourages more aggressive play. Holding the toy by your fingertips is a good way to manage the pressure.

6. When your puppy wins the toy, encourage him back to teach him that playing is more about having fun together than possession.

7. If the game shifts from fun interaction to possession of the toy, then stop playing for a while.

8. Always try to calm the playing down before you stop. It's disappointing stopping a game when it's at its most exciting.

9. And always end playtime on a good note. If you've had to stop for a moment, restart the game and end it when things are quiet and friendly.

22. PUPPY-PEOPLE TRANSLATOR

Your dog understands your every word, or so it's said. But however much truth there is in that, your choice of words is very important. Even more important though is how you say them. Be gentle but firm, patient, loving, encouraging, reassuring.

It is also said that a dog can say more with his tail in just a few seconds than its owner can say in hours, and you're no doubt already familiar with some of his more common expressions like, "I am so happy to see you!" and "You are the best thing that ever happened to me!"

In the very first days of getting your puppy, you

will have learned, "Your face is like a lovely lolly!" and when he is a bit older you are highly likely to come across a Jack Russell favourite, "Your training is coming along very nicely!"

A lot of your puppy's body language is really easy to read, but the signs are not always straightforward. A wagging tail can mean your puppy is happy, aggressive or excited, so we need to look at the whole picture including how he wags it and what else is going on around him at the time. To help with this, here are some English–Jack Russell translations:

I love you
    – Racing to meet you
    – Wagging tail
    – Licking
    – Whimpering

I'm so happy and excited
    – Tail wagging fast (but watch out. This can also be a sign of concentration or aggression)
    – Racing around
    – Whimpering
    – Pulling lips back and exposing teeth

Let's play
    – Jumping in front of you, facing you, front legs splayed out
    – Wagging tail vigorously
    – Rolling head
    – Dashing off and jumping back again

I hear something unusual. What is it? Where is it coming from?
– Head tilted to the side
– Brow raised
– Ears twitch and nose wiggles
– Mouth may be open and panting
– One paw raised

I'm totally chilled
– Lying on back with his legs flopped out
– Curled in a ball
– Lying down watching you

Feeling submissive
– Rolling over onto back, exposing tummy and genitals.
– Tail between legs
– Head dipped or tucked in, ears pinned back

I'm curious, and maybe also a little concerned, about something going on
– Raised paw

I'm frightened or unhappy
– Tail between legs
– Cowering, or lying down
– Ears twitching back and forth
– Staring ahead at object of fear
– Lying down with paws ahead,

looking ahead, ready to run
- Hackles raised on back
- Whining
- Whimpering
- Looking to you for help

I'm in pain or frightened and need your help

- Looking from you to whatever it is he needs, and then quickly back again
- Whining
- Whimpering

This is not manipulation. It's a genuine plea for help. Reassure him. Tell him that you hear him, you are there for him and he can count on you.

Aggressive

- Standing up straight
- Ears pinned back, or sharply forward
- Hackles (hairs on his back) raised
- Eyes fixed in a stare
- Body is tense, ready to attack
- Tail wagging in stiff, quick, stilted movements
- Barking

I'm warning you
- Snarling
- Growling
- Baring fangs
He should never do any of these at you. Only for you – to protect you and the family.

I'm sending out a warning, or locating other dogs because I'm feeling lonely
- Howling
- Baying

I want attention: 'hello', 'look at me', 'I'm bored'
- Barking at you

I'm begging you. Pleeez!
- Whining, with pleading eyes
Yes it's a heart-wrenching expression, but don't give in to that cute little face. Your environment will help you to tell the difference between begging and 'I'm in pain or frightened and want your help'. If you're eating a juicy steak that he's hoping you'll share, it's safe to assume he's begging.

23. STANDOUT JACK RUSSELLS

NIPPER

The logo for His Master's Voice (now HMV) features a dog listening to a phonograph. This is thought to be of Nipper, a Jack Russell-type dog born in 1884.

BOTHY

Bothy, owned by explorers Ranulph and Ginny Fiennes, made history in 1982 when he became the first dog to travel to both the North and South Poles.

GEORGE

In 2007, a Jack Russell called George saved five children at a fair in New Zealand from an attack by two pit bulls. He charged at them and held them at bay long enough for the children to get away, but died in the fight. A statue has been erected in his memory.

UGGIE

Uggie started his long acting career appearing in commercials in 2005. In 2011 he was cast in *The Artist* and *Water for Elephants,* and a campaign was launched to consider him for an Academy Award. Uggie was also named Nintendo's first spokesdog.

CHALKY

Well-recognised star Chalky belonged to restaurateur

and chef Rick Stein and frequently stole the show on his cookery series. Before long, he had his own line of merchandise and two award-winning ales names after him, 'Chalky's Bite' and 'Chalky's Bark'.

MOOSE AND ENZO

This father and son team shared the role of Eddie in the TV sitcom *Frasier*. They also stared as Skip in the 2000 film *My Dog Skip*.

SOCCER

Wishbone, from the TV show of the same name, was played by a Jack Russell named Soccer.

BEAR

The 1995 movie *Crimson Tide* featured Gene Hackman with this smooth-coated Jack Russell as his pet.

MAX

This little movie star played Milo, one of Stanley's only friends, in *The Mask* with Jim Carrey. Max also played Audrey, a female dog, in the film *Mr. Accident*.

COSMO

Friday, one of the main characters in the movie *Hotel for Dogs*, is played by Cosmo, a famous Jack Russell who went on to feature in the films *Beginners* and *Paul Blart: Mall Cop*.

'JACK RUSSELL'

Jack Russell: Dog Detective is a series of children's books featuring a Jack Russell called 'Jack Russell' as the main character.

EARL

The comic strip *Mutts* by Patrick McDonnell features a Jack Russell named Earl as the main character.

YOURS TRULY [_____]

Because I know you have invited a very special Jack Russell into your home. Thank you for wanting to be a good Jack Russell owner, and I hope this book will help get your new relationship off to the best possible start.

24. GOING FORWARD

Somewhere between five months and a year your puppy will go through adolescence which is usually the most difficult period for owners. He is growing in independence; his chewing continues relentlessly; and he will become more territorial. Hopefully the solid foundations you've laid in the early weeks and months will make this stage a little less wearing. Remind yourself it is short-lived.

Your puppy is also beginning to show the onset of sexual maturity. Females will come into season and males will experience huge fluctuations in male hormone levels, both of which will affect their behaviour. Most dogs go off exploring at this stage because they want to mate. If you're not planning on breeding, then having your Jack Russell neutered (spayed or castrated) can be the answer to the problem.

Spaying your female dog

Spaying not only prevents unwanted pregnancies and stops your dog from coming into season – which involves bleeding for up to three weeks in every six months – but it also stops her from trying to escape to find a mate; keeps persistent male dogs from pursuing her;

and reduces the risk of a number of health problems. The main disadvantage is that she may become prone to weight gain, but this is nothing that can't be controlled by a sensible diet and sufficient exercise. The recommended timing for spaying is either before her first season (which could be any time from six months to around 15 months) or two to three months after her season.

Castrating your male dog

Neutering not only prevents accidental breeding, it also reduces aggressiveness; undesirable sexual behaviour; urine marking; running off; and the risk of a number of health problems.

The best time for neutering varies from dog to dog and depending on who you ask. This is because it's important to get the balance right with your individual dog between physical growth and emotional maturity. Ideally you should wait until your puppy has reached its full frame size which, for a Jack Russell, is generally between six and eight months of age. (They tend to reach their full weight by a year.) You should also wait for signs of maturity – less bounce and reduced chewing are good indicators.

If your puppy is running off, or taking an overactive interest in the opposite sex – or its bedding, toys or even people's legs – it's probably time to speak to your vet.

Running off

If your puppy starts running off, which is most likely because he wants to mate, and this behaviour persists, you will need to keep him inside or in a fully-enclosed garden or yard, and while walking out he will need to stay on the lead.

But prevention is always the better option. If he does run off, be sure to praise him when he comes home. Never scold him when he is coming towards you, because in coming back to you he is being a good puppy. That way he will want to stay home and, even if he does run off again, he will always want to return.

The crate

When your puppy is toilet trained and has stopped eating everything in sight, you will be able to start leaving the crate door open. In the meantime, make sure you praise him when you see him going in on his own.

Feeding

Your puppy can move on to adult food between nine months old and a year. By then you will also be able to cut feeds back from three times to twice a day.

Training and dog sports

This book sets out to answer the most important early-stage questions on owning a Jack Russell puppy. It covers the things you need to know when he is still very young – the things you don't want to get wrong in his vital first months.

At a later stage you choose to fine-tune your training or need to deal with specific behavioural issues that could've arisen, and there are some excellent and extremely thorough books in the market.

And if you've got the time and inclination for obedience training classes, they are incredibly enriching for both you and your dog and he would love you for taking him, forever and more.

If you want to get more serious about play, consider enrolling your puppy in Flyball classes when he is older. Flyball is a team sport in which dogs race over hurdles to a box with a spring-loaded pad that releases a ball.

25. THERE WILL BE TIMES ...

This book is intended as an easy read to offer you some shortcuts with the theory. But there are NO short cuts with the practice. The practice needs patience and repetition, encouragement and reward.

Jack Russells are often too clever and too cute for their own good; have more courage than sense; and need more stimulation that we feel we can give. They are cheeky little monkeys as a rule. But that's why we like them, so remember this when you feel your patience running thin.

Hard times

There will be times when your puppy does all sorts of things you don't want him to. He will poop on the carpet; bark when he has something to say; whine when he's upset or lonely; and chew things when he's bored or teething.

Your house will be littered with toys, and the tick-tack of little paws will be under you feet when you go to the fridge, the toilet, the shower and the front door.

At some point you will be at your wits' end and you will look at him and think, "What have I got myself into?"

Good times

Don't try to make him more human because, just as he is, you will also have more love than you could ever imagine, and there will be way more times when you think, "How did I get so lucky?".

Your family has grown by four furry feet and when you walk through the door, your new best friend is waiting to greet you, ecstatic to see you. He will enrich your life with his unconditional love and loyalty, gratitude and forgiveness, help and protection, and buckets and buckets of laughs.

There will be plenty of times when he does the things you DO want him to do. Praise him – with attention, treats, toys … it doesn't matter what, as long as it's something he loves.

Taking-him-for-granted times

And last, but definitely not least, there will be times when he just IS – a calm, quiet presence by your side. Those are the times when it will be easiest for you to forget or ignore him, and those are the times when it is most important of all to remind yourself, and him, just how special he is.

Remember the saying, "Once you get a Jack, you never go back." Well, I haven't. Because they are simply fantastic little dogs. I want to thank the Jack Russells who've inspired this book, and give my best wishes to the ones this book inspires. May the information in these pages help to give Jack Russells everywhere the best possible start in life.

26. USEFUL CONTACTS

American Kennel Club
www.akc.org/dog-breeds/russell-terrier/

Animal Health Trust
www.aht.org.uk

Australian National Kennel Council
Ankc.org.au

Company of Animals
Companyofanimals.co.uk

Happy Jack Russell (Blog site)
www.happyjackrussell.com

Jack Russell Terrier Club of America
www.therealjackrussell.com

Kennel Union of Southern Africa
www.kusa.co.za

The British Jack Russell Terrier Club
britishjackrussellclub.com

The Kennel Club (UK)
www.thekennelclub.org.uk

INDEX